REAL PHONIES
AND
GENUINE FAKES

Also by Nicky Beer

The Octopus Game
The Diminishing House

REAL PHONIES AND GENUINE FAKES

poems **NICKY BEER**

MILKWEED EDITIONS

Published 2022 by Milkweed Editions
Printed in the United States of America
Cover design by Mary Austin Speaker
Cover art by Dane Shue
22 23 24 25 26   5 4 3 2 1
First Edition

Library of Congress Cataloging-in-Publication Data

Names: Beer, Nicky, author.

Title: Real phonies and genuine fakes : poems / Nicky Beer.

Description: First Edition. | Minneapolis, Minnesota : Milkweed Editions, 2022. | Summary: "With an energetic eye, Nicky Beer thumbs through our collective history books-and her personal one, too-in an effort to chart the line between playful forms of farce and those that are far more insidious"-- Provided by publisher.

Identifiers: LCCN 2021031223 (print) | LCCN 2021031224 (ebook) | ISBN 9781571315397 (trade paperback) | ISBN 9781571317490 (ebook)

Subjects: LCGFT: Poetry.

Classification: LCC PS3602.E363 R43 2022   (print) | LCC PS3602.E363 (ebook) | DDC 811/.6--dc23

LC record available at https://lccn.loc.gov/2021031223

LC ebook record available at https://lccn.loc.gov/2021031224

Milkweed Editions is committed to ecological stewardship. We strive to align our book production practices with this principle, and to reduce the impact of our operations in the environment. We are a member of the Green Press Initiative, a nonprofit coalition of publishers, manufacturers, and authors working to protect the world's endangered forests and conserve natural resources. *Real Phonies and Genuine Fakes* was printed on acid-free 100% postconsumer-waste paper by McNaughton & Gunn.

For Maya—always genuine, always real.

CONTENTS

Drag Day at Dollywood | 1
Self-Portrait as Duckie Dale | 3
Cathy Dies | 4
Two-Headed Taxidermied Calf | 6
Etymology | 8
Still Life with Pork Livers Rolled Like Handkerchiefs | 9
Thorn Ostinato | 11

Marlene Dietrich Plays Her Musical Saw for the Troops, 1944 | 15
Forged Medieval German Church Fresco with Clandestine
        Marlene Dietrich | 16
The Benevolent Sisterhood of Inconspicuous Fabricators | 18
The Magicians at Work | 19
Sawing a Lady in Half | 20
The Great Something | 21
The Plagiarist | 22
Notes on the Village of Liars | 23
Excerpts from *The Updated Handbook to Mendacity* | 24

The Stereoscopic Man | 28

Self-Portrait While Operating Heavy Machinery | 43
The Demolitionists | 44
Small Claims Courtship | 45
Exclusive Interview | 46
Marlene Dietrich Meets David Bowie, 1978 | 49
Marlene Dietrich Considers Penicillin, 1950 | 50
Mating Call of the Re-Creation Panda | 52
Scat | 53
Heart in Turmeric | 56

𝄡

Dear Bruce Wayne, | 61
Elegy | 63
Kindness/Kindling | 65
Juveniles | 66
Nessun Dorma | 67
The Poet Who Does Not Believe in Ghosts | 69
Because my grief was a tree | 71
Specimen #17 | 72
Revision | 73

Notes | 75
Acknowledgments | 77

You shouldn't let poets lie to you.

—Björk

REAL PHONIES
AND
GENUINE FAKES

Drag Day at Dollywood

. . . some of them look more like me than I do.
—Dolly Parton

Blue beehives whirl and loopily ascend
long paper wands. Candied apples smash into
shades of Vixen, Strike Me Pink, Cherries in the Snow.
Lamé by the square mile ripples under the Tennessee sun.
From a distance, the Mountain Sidewinder looks like a drunk,
bejeweled caterpillar. The screams sound the same as on any other day.
By closing time, seven hundred and eighty-two press-on nails
will have been lost. A few contrarians bust out their best
Patsys or Lorettas, dark bouffants stippling
the deluge of blonde. Someone's great-aunt
comes as Kenny Rogers and strokes her beard
like a newly-adopted lapdog. A bus from Atlanta
unleashes two dozen Dollys in matching bowling jackets,
Gutter Queens sprawled across their backs in lilac script.
To relieve the boredom at the Mystery Mine line,
someone hollers *"When I say 'Homo' you say 'Sapiens.'"*
"HOMO!" "SAPIENS!" "HOMO!" "SAPIENS!"
Dollys line the perimeter of the bald eagle sanctuary,
watching the raptors swoop stoically on the other side
of the netted enclosure. *"They mate for life!"* Dolly exclaims,
reading from Wikipedia on her phone. *"Awww,"* Dolly says.
"Ughhh," says Dolly. A tall Dolly gives a short Dolly
a piggyback ride through Jukebox Junction, making
a laughing, lumbering chimera of poly satin and fringe.
Dolly holds back Dolly's hair as she vomits purple
slush and kettle corn into a bank of azaleas.
Dolly, with weary patience, explains to Dolly

1

why she can't pet her service dog. Dollys grasp
turkey legs in their fists, tear flesh from bone.
Thousands of pairs of Dolly lungs breathe in
gasoline and grease, breathe out glitter. Dolly
visits the restroom to check her wig and loses
track of herself in the mirrors. Dolly drifts
along an automated river, an undiagnosed tumor
humming gently under her lifejacket. Dolly
holds a thumb and forefinger up to the setting sun,
pinches it, and lovingly places it in Dolly's back pocket.
Dolly, exhausted and sunburned, collapses
onto a bench, rests her head on Dolly's breast,
who rests her head on Dolly's breast, who rests
her head on Dolly's breast on Dolly's breast.

Self-Portrait as Duckie Dale

Pretty in Pink (1986)

It was always me in that shaggy suit jacket,
the battered dance shoes, the fuck-you-rich-boy
pompadour. When you cannot wail
your rain-shot, neon-blasted love
to the red-headed girls of the world,
Otis Redding is your only recourse,
your body rigid with borrowed soul.
Who knows better than another woman
to try a little tenderness?
Only the weary girls understand this.
Only the ones making knife-brimmed style
from what the dead throw away.
Only the ones with a ready wisecrack
for each of the thousand heartbreaks
that crackle across the unrequited radio.
Dames, we sigh, sipping the long light
in the unmowed front yard,
our hidden breasts swaying under
secondhand shirts like palm trees.
Isn't she—? asks the light. *Isn't she*, we reply.

Cathy Dies

You haven't killed yourself because you'd have to
commit to a single exit. What you wouldn't give
to be your cousin Catherine, who you'd watched twice
in one weekend get strangled nude in a bathtub onstage
by the actor who once filled your pre-teen fevers
with lush-lipped Britishisms. Backstage, he talked to you
without his hairpiece and was unafraid of how your eyes
measured his skull. *Law & Order: Criminal Intent* put her
severed head in a bucket, pulling the towel back
on her clotted bangs a second before the cut
to Honda's Year End Clearance Event.
And you swear that was her Cygnus-tattooed calf flailing
on the Syfy Network as the mutated piranhas
swarmed like sexed-up galoshes. Some days,
you're convinced she's the blur of the passerby behind
the city comptroller interviewed on the 11 o'clock news,
the last lighted window squinting on the high-rise,
the silhouette the pigeons spatter over
the elevated subway platform in Astoria where the bakery
underneath releases the ache of its scent
which anyone it touches will eventually die from—
the ache of how it can do nothing but ascend.
She's been nominated for an Emmy for her portrayal of
the concerned line between your doctor's eyebrows
as he listened to the giant, sodden moth trapped
between your shoulders, the ruin you carry
around with you like a speech you're always prepared
to give. How you're prepared to be Woman at Bottom of Ravine,
T.O.D. Unknown, Woman Found in Motel Room

and It's a Goddamned Shame, Understudy to Woman
Overdosing, Woman in the Prop Photo in the Wallet
Catherine takes out of her coat and lays gently on the balustrade
before the black sky pours down its scroll of names.

Two-Headed Taxidermied Calf

Deer Trail Pioneer Historical Museum, Colorado

I hated myself for pitying it—
nearly thirty years dead, and alive
for only a few hours—
as if that could do any good.
But there was something
in its tender swirls of ochre hair
that the amateur taxidermist
couldn't quite make
laughable. Yes, the eyes
were badly-shaped, but I almost
believed them anyway. When they cut
the mother open, did the mouths bawl
in unison or harmony?
Did the lungs fill twice as fast?
I tried to convince myself
none of it was real, not even
the notarized signatures
of the rancher and vet,
remembering that faking provenance
is a hoax's easiest gamble.
I thought of the days before the pills,
and the large stone my bad chemicals made
for me to carry, a secret
sideshow attraction
to myself: *The Woman Who Smiles.*
Step right up and observe her
perfect imitation of a person
who doesn't want to die.

Caesar was a twin, the other
stillborn. They say
he believed if he swept
his arm across enough of the world,
he'd finally catch the brother
who'd abandoned him to dream
alone in the dark. I reached past
the display's blunted barbed wire
to stroke one coarse flank.
When the animal was dying,
was it relieved it wasn't dying
alone? Did all four eyes close
at the same time, two final streams
of milk-breath leaking
into the early prairie light?
I lied before, about Caesar
being born a twin. Sorry.
I just wanted to see
if I was still as good at it
as I used to be.
To see if I could still
smooth a little poison
over glass and polish it
to a diverting flash,
a mirror showing everything
but itself.

Etymology

Those were the days when I didn't want to kill myself but I did take the word *suicide* out of my pocket now and then, its syllables like the undulations of black and orange furred caterpillars, revolting and adorable. Sometimes the word would grow tender rows of quills that I could stroke and pluck into a private music. Even the abysmal eyes of horses watching me as I walked through their country of flies could not silence it. I was the man in his dead mother's summer dress preening over one shoulder in a hand mirror, admiring how his dark hair foamed at the décolletage, waiting for the annihilating footstep on the stair.

Still Life with Pork Livers Rolled Like Handkerchiefs

Western Daughters Butcher Shoppe, Denver

Their color, not of blood,
but blood's blood,
whatever courses deeper
within its oiled music.
Blister. Boil. Blemish.
Red of the body turning
furious when there is no path
out of itself. Red of the insides
of the blue guitar, the taste
of the inside of my tongue.
If I could turn on the light
behind my closed eyelids.
If I could make the mosquito's
stolen feast speak. God,
the loneliness of red,
the airplane's blinking eye
above the indifferent world,
the plaint of the buoy in chop.
Those sea anemone mouths
of pigflesh poised to kiss
nothing. And yet they make
me want to be cleavered and trimmed,
to be made more
tidy than I ever was
while living. To be priced,
made sense of by the pound,
wrapped in blank paper,
sent off to dozens

of different tables to be
overcooked, badly garnished,
casseroled into leftovers,
sneaked in bits to the dog,
partially forgotten
at the back of the fridge,
furred blue with mold.
To not know, in the end,
if I was good.
Only that I was filling.

Thorn Ostinato

O rose your shag and slather of sweet
O rose the parrot-chirp of my shears as I behead you each dusk
O rose the half-sketched map you make on my forearms
O rose the palsied raccoon smells my skin on your incisors
O rose we prune each other
O rose you lay your dozens of white tongues on mine
O rose your drugged bees that stumble into my hair
O rose for a throat as green and pliant as yours
O rose your bleak brown bones in my fist
O rose you coral reef in the night's undertow
O rose you brain of ravenous aphids
O rose you etymology in the unspeakable summer
O rose the salacious vine strangles you sans malice
O rose the black wind shatters your face
O rose the black wind shatters my face
O rose show me how to die in all directions

Marlene Dietrich Plays Her Musical Saw for the Troops, 1944

See how the silver snaps in a lone spot,
the sound flirting with coyotes,
castrated foghorns, distant siren.
Observe how that polished body curves
in the strategy of lights, how its voice
is like a parody of mourning,
and so even more mournful
immersed in its high-pitched joke.
Admit that some other instrument
would fail—wood-honeyed curve,
funneled brass—when what's needed
now is a tongue with the chill of steel.
Watch how the thighs hold that music
steady, how the dust and moths draw
closer to the song, a song that's dying
even as it hovers in the dark,
a lost mouth moaning vowels
that are too close to your name.

Forged Medieval German Church Fresco with Clandestine Marlene Dietrich

after Lothar Malskat (1913–1988)

> . . . *Malskat was outraged when no one believed that he had painted what*
> *seemed to be newly discovered medieval frescoes in a German church. Even*
> *when he pointed out the [anachronisms] he had inserted (a painting of a turkey*
> *which, being indigenous to North America, had not been seen in Europe in the*
> *Middle Ages, and a portrait of Marlene Dietrich, who definitely had not been*
> *seen in Europe in the Middle Ages), no one believed him.*
>
> —Noah Charney

You can hardly blame Malskat for making her
a small part of his fraud. She seemed to come
from a time before the third dimension
in portraiture was invented—all brusque
slashes of eyebrows, cheekbones, mouth.
As if she were meant to live only on surfaces
lit by fire or candlelight, smoke inscribing
its restless dialects across her forehead.
She was a brief kiss he blew to himself
while shaping the rest of the fake saints he'd claimed
to uncover after cleaning the true ones
on another wall, a little insurance in case he'd need
to later claim it all a joke, his painterly harm less
evil than the supercilious experts who'd burnished his lie.
Which is to say, a prop. A stolen bit of her face,
lunar and lonely, to better light his ego's way.
Which is to say, for his love of himself, and not her.
But didn't she deserve, a little bit, to be used?
Didn't she terrify us with the weight of our desire,
then fail us in being mortal? Didn't she bring

her slow withering in the dark down on herself
with her own bitch-hand, grasping and ungovernable?
Beauty should always taste a bit of its own blood
and blame in its teeth. Shouldn't she pay
for making us want? Listen to how our prayers
fill in the space of whatever she'd have chosen
to say. Tell me we don't want all our goddesses
flattened and pinned to a wall, wings spread
and immobile. Tell me time doesn't feed
on a woman face-first. Tell me we don't love
her expression when she sees she can't
get out of the killing jar.

The Benevolent Sisterhood of Inconspicuous Fabricators

The list of famous forgers is long and virtually entirely male.
—Edward Dolnick, *The Forger's Spell*

The matron greets you at the front door with a stern eye, chewing on the thin stem of a clay pipe. In the later hours, with a more than a little absinthe, she'll regale you with the saltier tales of the models she used for her Rodins: "Torsos and haunches for months, love!" As you sign in, you hear someone holler from an upper floor: "Bernice, you cunt, did you steal my fucking ultramarine again?" The air is redolent with linseed oil and cooking custard. As the matron mounts the steps ahead of you, you see the veins climbing her calves like tree branches springing from Baroque marble.

Second floor studios are reserved for bibliofraud. You look in on a young woman with a strong jaw milking ink from a cuttlefish sac. Her neighbor squints over the margins of a yellowing folio through a blue monocle. A butter-colored python snoozes across her shoulders. You mistake the wallpaper in one room for a deranged set of optometrist's charts, until you recognize them as trials of Gothic calligraphy. "Did a few Biblical apocrypha, that one," she nods to the resident, who tips her iron-streaked topknot towards you, in which a goose feather quivers. On the fourth floor, a redhead snores face-down on a palette, the light through the closed curtains catching a smear of white across her nose. In the corridor, a woman with a pinched, church-lady face brushes by. "Modigliani sketches. Fantastic tits—models them after her girlfriend's."

Your legs are just starting to ache as you reach the top floor. "Lord!" the matron groans as she grasps the newel post. Some joker has carved RUSKIN WAS HERE into the scarred wood. "Well, ducky, this is you," she says as she unlocks the room. You set your bags down on the bare floor, tip her, and listen to her step shudder its way back down the stairs. You brush a dead fly off the windowsill, crack your knuckles. Your masterpieces will never be yours again.

The Magicians at Work

after Jim Steinmeyer's book Hiding the Elephant: How Magicians
Invented the Impossible and Learned to Disappear

Over the years they hunted,
the wayward apprentice watchmakers,
the disappointing sons who transformed
their surnames, hunted over acres
of hinges, cogs, calluses, hidden whiskey,
mustaches a breath from feral,
poured an ocean of fortune
into fabrications of brass and iron,
spent entire seasons strumming
massive harps of wire into perfect
calibrations of invisibility,
prayed to the gods of adjustable mirrors,
cursed the gods of temperamental gaslights,
broke the legs of imitators and thieves,
chewed holes in each other's pockets,
harnessed nightmares of giant silver hoops
making endless passes over the bodies
of the dead, hoisted high a cenotaph
for hundreds of sacrificed rabbits,
breathed miles of delicate thread
into the lost labyrinths of their lungs,
all to make a woman float
to make a woman float
and none of them ever thought
of simply asking her.

Sawing a Lady in Half

they want it to be true
and don't want it to be true
that they want it to be true

The Great Something

A pair of white cotton gloves rests on an empty wooden chair, as if awaiting an absent butler. The magician elaborately blots his tongue with a red bandana, blindfolds himself. An assistant cuffs his hands while a volunteer from the audience writes a single word of their choosing on a small piece of paper, then dons the gloves. An onstage camera projects the word on a screen so that the audience can see it, make note of the handwriting: crabbed and cranky W's, T's slashed with drunkenly unbalanced bars, O's missing the tops of their skulls. The magician opens his mouth, and the volunteer folds the paper and places it inside. The magician closes his mouth, and a twenty-second drumroll—added to the act at the behest of the manager—commences. After the percussive flourish, the magician opens his mouth, and the paper, like a wayward, solitary moth emerging from behind his teeth, is visible again. The volunteer removes it, opens it, reads it. Now the need for the onstage chair is made plain: the volunteer must sit down. On the paper is an entirely different word—still written in their own handwriting. *Water* has become *money*. *Mother* has become *assassin*. The assistant gently asks them to verify that this is, in fact, their own script. The volunteer nods weakly, and the assistant holds the slip up to the camera so that the crowd may see. *Wednesday* has become *elephant*. *Infect* has become *angel*. Small Rorschachs of saliva bloom around the word. The volunteer's face looks as if they'd been shown a photograph of themselves taken while sleeping in an empty house. *It was a wonderful trick*, the manager recalls, years later, *and people applauded, but they hated it. Steal their wallets, turn their wedding rings into eggs—they don't mind. But this was something else. When he was found in that awful state, with what they'd done to his mouth—well, no one was really surprised. But don't quote me on that.*

The Plagiarist

I only steal from the ones
you've never heard of,
the ones whose fingers
shook too hard to hold
a pen, the ones who froze
with their heads to the ground
like cattle in a blizzard,
the ones who drowned
like witches in their sleep.
One I shut up in a closet
and fed through the keyhole:
spoonfuls of broth
in exchange for genius.
Another I hypnotized
into thinking she was a bird,
charmed her with seeds
each morning to my bed.
Her little claws clutched
my nipples, and she couldn't keep
her songs inside her.
For one, I had to rummage
in his torso, elbow-deep.
I found his words folded beneath
his sweetbread, nodes draped
like a yellow quilt. The flies took
up the conversation from there.

Notes on the Village of Liars

after Jenny George

Sunrise arrives just as it would anywhere.

A raccoon sleeps in the dry fountain of the main square.

Children drag dark red jump ropes along the streets behind them.

There is a local motto, but no one can quite remember what it is. Something
       to do with persistence.

Beekeeping is a popular pastime. There is always enough smoke and honey.

The shadow of the tallest building resembles a broken arm.

A feather is nailed upside-down above every doorway. This symbolizes a
       tongue.

Don't ask me how they determined the correct direction of the feather.

A guard is always posted at the cemetery, because who knows for sure?

Everyone is the mayor. No one is the executioner.

Every book has been stolen from a library somewhere else.

Yes, even this one.

Excerpts from *The Updated Handbook to Mendacity*

The lie

you write with a pencil.

you write with a stolen pen.

you'd stitched into the lining of a coat you donated to the church
rummage sale.

you tell to the teacup when it asks where its saucer is.

you fatten on corn in your cellar.

you wrap in a silk handkerchief and bury in your neighbor's yard.

you dress up like your wife and take to brunch.

The lie

you split down its length, from which you extract burning seeds with
the tip of your knife.

you leave undusted like a hated figurine.

The lie

you leave between pages 258 and 259 of *The History of the Magna
Carta* in the library of a small town in Indiana.

you whisper into the divot of your mother's inoculation scar.

you tell the centipede living in your wallet.

you try to rhyme with *harmless*.

The lie
you pay someone else to tell you.

you devour in a hungry unthinking handful.

you forget you've told before, but this time you tell it to his brother.

you tell the dentist as the smell of drilled bone vaporizes into the
ceiling.

The lie
you make with maps.

you make with surnames.

you tell with *maybe*.

you tell while showing your empty hands.

The Stereoscopic Man

after Magritte

stereoscope: An optical instrument through which two slightly different images (typically photographs) of the same scene are presented, one to each eye, providing an illusion of three dimensions.

—*The American Heritage Science Dictionary*

INTRODUCING THE STEREOSCOPIC MAN

He is neither	the man
on the right nor	the left
Inside one	eye drowns a
thumbprint	Blue
spectacles	echo
nothing	he doesn't see
Opening	the door
for himself	he cannot
move	for sheer courtesy:
«Après	vous.» «Pas du tout—
Après	vous.»

THE STEREOSCOPIC MAN CONSIDERS HIS ORIGINS

He doesn't know   how he happened
Perhaps one of him   is the new claw
the lobster resurrects   from its wound
The dual-sexed   worm-halves
moseying   in opposite
directions   from their old self
The sea sponge   pinching off
its own face   for company
The blood   estuaries
the sea made   to call
endlessly back   to itself
from inside   us

THE STEREOSCOPIC MAN TAKES A LOVER

It's an orgy   with the mirror
in the room   She asks it
to tell her   whose shoulder
she has   between her
teeth   Or could it be
her own   Is the ceiling
getting   closer
Whose name   is being
moaned   against
the mattress   Why
did the blinds   stroke their
shadows over her   mons
When   did she come
How   did she come
Who   did she come

SOMETHING THE STEREOSCOPIC MAN SAYS (SUBTITLED)

"Did you say   something?"
"Yes. Did you   say something?"
"Yes. Did you?"   "Yes."

THE STEREOSCOPIC MAN AND BINOCULAR VISION

What's there
through the lenses is
fraud
on your eyes'
It's a science film
where mitosis
and the twin cells
of cytokinesis
into their
Their history
folds away

when you peer
a three-dimensional
a con that thrives
bumpkin trust
run backwards
is reversed
forget the grief
Dissolving back
singular mother
of multiplicity
into her loving nucleus

THE KINDERGARTENER TALKS TO THE STEREOSCOPIC MAN

My mom says   *I need to wear*
these because   *I have bad*
death   *perception*

SEGAL'S LAW AND THE STEREOSCOPIC MAN

A man with one watch always knows what time it is,
and a man with two watches is never sure.

The man with two hearts: always a little out of love.
The man with two mouths: a breath away from a lie.
The man with two spines: never at rest.
The man with two moons: howling and about to howl.
The man with two birthdays: late for everything.
The man with two noses: snubs himself.
The man with two navels: impossible to untie from his fate.
The man with two signatures: owner of nothing.
The man with two autumns: never enough regret.

THE STEREOSCOPIC MAN'S LAST WILL AND TESTAMENT

To my heirs   *I leave*
my right   *to what*
is left   *of me*

THE STEREOSCOPIC MAN DREAMS OF BELUGA WHALES

The cetaceans engage in hemispheric sleep:
one half of the brain at rest
the other with its periscope
propped up to the world the body swaying
like a loose crescent moon each dream
twitching a fluke waving to itself
a mirror on the other side of an unsafe bridge

THE STEREOSCOPIC MAN TALKS TO HIMSELF IN THE CAVE

Is he the echo   The echo is he

THE STEREOSCOPIC MAN WATCHES *IT CAME FROM OUTER SPACE* IN 3-D

No red and blue glasses needed
He raises all of his eyes
to everything that came from
outer space a past vision of the future
in opalescent obsolescence a theremin whine
The aliens shift their bodies
into duplicates of us
drift out into the desert while their ship's cleaved
hull grins darkly In the last reel
copies and originals briefly come face to face
share a glance in a shadowed cave
before the aliens shift back
into their single-eyed selves
He applauds with one hand

SUIS-SOMME

He writes   a strongly-worded postcard
to Science   petitioning for the creation
of nomenclature   for the moment
when a splitting   cell first thinks
I am   *we.*

HOW HE READS

Recto and verso simultaneously
out of order Past and future
a stew of present tense
Cause and effect a perverse erasure
without consequences
Epiphanies springing from nothing
This is how he came to believe
in God in God

Self-Portrait While Operating Heavy Machinery

I brandish the chainsaw in the deadgrass field,
make it swoop the air in snarling, oily ellipses.
From a distance, we look like a convulsing ostrich.
The secret about the pills is that they're completely harmless;
the real danger is what I'll do when I'm not afraid of anything,
The Bureau of My Assured Future Failures
placed on furlough, offices shuttered, *I Told You So*
rubber stamps gathering dust, *Yes You Can't* banner sagged
and partially unstrung in the break room. Listen
to how quiet it is when I lose the self-doubt played
for so long I mistook it for music. I'm crowned
with welding sparks as I drape dull jewels of dynamite
over the throats of town square statues, as I turn
a sliding panel van into my own personal tank.
But wait. Let's go back to that field where I'm swinging
the chainsaw. Such joyful, hazardous arcs
you've never seen. I'm slicing up huge chunks of the sky
to stack and burn for the winter, not a single tree left.

The Demolitionists

In my latest dream,
instead of having sex, we blow up buildings.
We take long walks down dusk-smudged streets, looking
like any other pair of lovers, sighing
up at the brownstones, the children's hospital:
This one? Oh, yes, that one. We carry a little
map and a red wax pencil with us
to remember. We return under cover
of night, press our dynamite
deep into the cracked walls. The cable snakes
behind us like the black, glistering wake
of a bad gondola. I'm in smart taffeta
and a veil, with a garnet cocktail ring
you cover like an eclipse
as you place your hand over mine
on the plunger. Later you'll gather me
a bouquet of rebar and brickdust,
a solemn snow of ex-phonebooks
and collection notices whitening the air.
But first, I count backwards
with the most incendiary words I know,
watch smoke trickle like lovescript
from your nose and ears.

Small Claims Courtship

I took the twenty-seven bones from my left hand
and made a xylophone on which to play
you love songs. I dragged a wheelbarrow
of sugar backwards over the parking lot
so the ants could spell out your name.
In your honor, I placed a respectable second
in the county fair's eel-eating contest. After my long-term
letter-writing campaign, Uruguay
has agreed to reclassify you as its national fern.
That easily-blackmailed cosmonaut
will be whispering blessings upon you
when she faces Jupiter. A kindergarten
in Duluth dreams only of your smile
at naptime. I'd rather not say how or why.
I've tuned the grackles to the key of your favorite jingle—
not perfectly, no. The world still fights me a little.
Let's not even mention the angle of that
cloud. I name my right shoe *twitterpated* and my left shoe
hopeless before I circle your mailbox each night.
My exhale is *symptom* and my inhale is *remedy*.

Exclusive Interview

██████████████████████████████████████?

People might be surprised to learn that, in certain cultures, the theft of a hat is considered to be a sign of respect. So given the circumstances, I think my actions were perfectly justified.

██████████████████████████████████?

Strawberries, hazelnuts, bee stings, 3 p.m. in November, a windy sigh issued by a man with an asymmetrical beard, nylon, certain varieties of cumulonimbus, and Bach's Sonata No. 2 in A Minor.

█████████████████████████████████?

Oh no—certainly not. Such organizations, with all their mystic rituals and mummery, really do more harm than good, don't you think? And the font on their application form is far too small.

████████████████████████████████████?

I would probably have to say my mother. She was a loving, tender-hearted woman, who always felt terrible when her divinations would keep us up at night, or if one of her numerous scabs fell into the porridge, or if her shoes would start walking about the house on their own. But no matter what demonspawn she might have been summoning, she was always there to meet us at the bus stop after school, discreetly wiping the viscera from her hands.

██████████ ?

Only once, and I have to say that I didn't care for it. You have to remember that in my day, only truckers and ornithologists did that sort of thing.

██
██
██
██
██
██
██████████████████ ?

Yes.

████████████████ ?

Shit-sucking-motherfucking-cock-gobbling-*cunt*! Oh wait—no. Capricorn.

██████████████████████████ ?

I think that's when my work really took off. Suddenly ordinary corridors became catacombs, their spaces reaching beyond themselves into the histories of the dead, where last words wait to be excavated from between long-abandoned teeth. No wonder the critics hated it.

██████████████████████████ ?

It's not so much that I regret it, it's that I wish I could pull certain years out of my body with a slim, silver hook, watching them painlessly emerge from my skin and dissolve like blue fog rising off a pond.

████████████████████████████ ?

I think the best piece of advice I've ever gotten was from ███ ███—she was a childhood friend of my aunt's, you know. She told me—this was before all that business about ████ and ████ in the ████ was made public—"never ████ a ██████ when you can ████ a larger ████." Words to live by.

Marlene Dietrich Meets David Bowie, 1978

on the set of Just a Gigolo

She knows at a glance that his suit's Saville Row;
he knows that her lipstick is Cherries in the Snow.

Marlene Dietrich Considers Penicillin, 1950

. . . and so it's decay that saves us, she thinks.
She presses her fingertips against her jaw,
pulls them away quickly, irritably,
snaps them in the air. Used to violets,
carnations, emeralds, any number of love-
tokens, this is the first to arrive in a Petri dish.
She'd already given it her body years ago
on the front lines in Italy, wild with fever
in between USO shows, the panzer blasts
and firefights shimmering into raucous neon
applause. She'd told Fleming all of this
when they'd dined, his wife retreating
into a bashful, bemused silence. *My dear,*
my dear, he'd murmured, the lenses
of his spectacles smoking and glinting
in the candlelight, though she was damned
to know if he'd meant her or the medicine.
She holds the dish to the light, catches
her reflection in its white constellations,
tilts it to a more flattering angle. She shrugs
at the doctor's note—*Some historical mold*
for a woman who's molded history—gently
amused by the schoolboy charm. Men her age
are called *fine specimens*. Women her age
simply aren't called. For a moment
she imagines a cool container
in which she could make a timeless world,
her body stilled and cellular, adored

by microscopes. *Bravo*, she murmurs,
pressing her lips to the glass, leaving
a red bird against the milky clouds,
somewhere between ascent and crash.

Mating Call of the Re-Creation Panda

after Melissa Milgrom

> "*Re-creations are defined as renderings which include NO natural parts of the animal portrayed. . . . For instance, a re-creation eagle could be constructed using turkey feathers, or a cow hide could be used to simulate African game.*"
> —World Taxidermy Championships rulebook

Cleanliness is my only real fault:
I could have done with a little faux-shit
yellowing my rump, something to make it
seem like the bamboo I'm chewing will end up
somewhere. I bear the bodies
of seventeen grizzlies on my back alone:
peeled, dried, Clairol-dyed and quilted
into the whole of me. I know that my ears
were done with great tenderness,
and one quiet evening, my maker even
briefly held one in his mouth.
That I have no memory is hardly his fault:
I'm not even a ghost, since this requires both
life and death as precedent. Says the poet:
What is more precise than precision? Illusion. I am more
precise than the clockwork of your own
expiring mitochondria. Come closer.
Try to guess the provenance of my claws,
gently blow the dust from the smoked snifters
of my eyes. Imagine from what, or whom,
your own body could be collaged, whose
lips could be stitched into an homage
of your smile. Take my lie in your arms.

Scat

for Brian

On the Sangre de Cristo trails
we found brazen, chalky discards,
the devoured bones turned to pressed powder
in the sun—the predator's signal
to its kind: *here I am*. This morning,
the spume of flies had drawn us
to the drying jumble outside the cabin
door. Stippled with indigo
berry seeds, matted fronds
of hair warped and whorled the leavings.
Tightly-wrapped bindle of hunger
that I poked and skewered with twigs,
as if I'd expected to find a fully-intact
murine glare: *take a picture*, etc.
I remember unscrambling the stories
buried in the owls' pellets,
a diagram of voles' bones grubbily taped
to my grade-school desk. No one
was ready to let Will Kiernan forget
how the rank tributary of diarrhea
had escaped the yellow poly hem
of his gym shorts during the spelling test
even though he'd begged Mrs. Ligouri
for a hall pass. Poor Shit Willie,
who crashed on the expressway
junior year a few weeks after
Denise had let him go to third.
And I told him I'd kill him if he told anyone,

she'd wept. I'd thought about killing
the goddamned hospice nurse
with the bad back when she called me
to the hospital bed in the living
room to help lift my mother
off the bedpan—my mother, who then took
my hand in hers, oversoft and moth-
colored, and raised it to her lips.
But it wasn't enough to make me forgive
the nurse, because Ma had already had enough
taken from her without seeing me
turn my head when her gown rode up.
And even though I'd grimaced
at the pile your old dog dropped,
as I knelt in the baked crabgrass
and for the first time closed my bagged hand
around the stinking warmth, I saw
the years together ahead of us as certainly
as he'd pulled me back home. . .
Whatever had looked in the wide glass
last night must have scented the mineral spatter
you'd sprawled across my belly,
cooled to scales as we dozed
in the leathered bulk of the sectional.
Only you could know that when
I say that rabbits will eat
the black cabochons of their own
turds—to ensure not a single nutrient
has been lost—I am talking love.
The glittering green-red bolide
that cleaved the sky for a few strange seconds,

searing the constellations we'd never learned
to name on that vast and empty plain—
only you could have known that
I would have opened my mouth to it
again and again.

Heart in Turmeric

after Nancy Bowen's Black Heart (2001)

The smell is why you enter the gallery.
You can't place it at first, but it scratches
at a memory lodged far back in a drawer,
a drawer that always sticks slightly,
narrow and deep like a trough.
Sunlight warming a secret
patch of dirt. A lover's armpit
in the roll and stretch
of an early morning dream. Blood
baking in your underwear.
At the center of the room, a heart
the size and color of a juvenile black bear
curled in sleep. Radiating from it
in a lopsided lagoon: yards
of turmeric, like the surface of a yellow planet.
Trenches of spice cupping yellow
shadows, hummocks arching and fat,
daring you to take a fistful.
You inhale and the yellow invades, pollinating
your tongue, clamoring your throat. Your lungs
become damp lanterns throwing out a yellow light.
It's like the opposite of disease. An orchestra
plays yellow music with sinew-chewed fingers
stained yellow, sheet music blooming
yolky fingerprints. *Yellow lives in the dark*,
you think, and don't know why. You know
what you want, though: to strip
and crawl through the spice slowly,

to approach the sleek heart and touch
your forehead to it in greeting, to roll,
to wallow up fragrant clouds, to be a wordless
beast coated in autumnal dust. To have
the fog furze and stain your sight.
You want your speech and sentiment gone,
your sympathies torn off like an old sheet.
You'd be happy to let the color—any color—
take over, to let what's left of you grind
down to pure flavor, something indelible
enough to haunt the floorboards right
down to their deepest grain, light enough
to be dispersed by the wind
of a door opening.

Dear Bruce Wayne,

My parents are dead, too.
A dirty, self-cannibalizing Gotham—
I also claim it, its city limits
built by my skin. I slough
and slough, but the city remains.
Tell me, if you'd watched
your mother's face go
a slow yellow after they cut
off her breast, if you'd watched
your father's mind get chewed down
to spasms, who would
you fight then? What broken
string of pearls would you chase
into the gutter? Lucky boy
to have an enemy.

*

Admit it—what bugs you
the most about the Joker
is his drag. You suspect
his crayoned mouth a lampoon
of your dead mother.
But don't you crave,
sometimes, to be a little
tacky? Doesn't the all-black
bore after a while?
Even your sweet ride can't help

but leave a little fart of flames
in its wake.
How many others
glare from the shadows
at a one-man parade
in a loud costume, blowing
glitter kisses at grim Justice?
You just think you want
to kill him for better reasons.
What kind of person would trade
laughter for righteousness?

*

Every woman goes out
knowing what you think
you alone had sussed:
the world is a dark alley
hiding a gun in its mouth.
It has more than enough
reasons to make you
cover your face.
The moon waxes. The bruise
wanes. Every woman
is Batman.

Elegy

I never liked the dead boy.
When the accident happened,
he became our parents' lessons
to us about being careful. They even
seemed to love him a little
for how useful he'd become.
I spent the school assembly
they gave him looking at the necks
of all the kids in front of me,
imagining a blue dot centered
on each one, like buttons
waiting to be jabbed.
The blow-up photo
had a dopey haze to it,
and he squinted back
at us as though through
a steambath of honey.
Everyone cried, even
the assistant principal he'd once
called a *Bitch* to her face.
Light peered through
the high windows' mesh,
stopped short in mid-
air, touching nothing
but a sullen ribbon
caught in the rafters,
dangling the rubber
of its spent balloon.

I already knew it
would never drop
in my lifetime.

Kindness/Kindling

Everyone loved the girl whose house burned down. The number of party invitations must have exhausted her, and we buried her under piles of new dolls and stuffed animals, which must have made it difficult for her to love any one of them especially. She was gravely awarded first sniff of the cherry magic marker. Class photo, front and center. Girl Whose House Burned Down for class president, Girl Whose House Burned Down for hall monitor, Girl Whose House Burned Down for kickball captain. We wished she'd broken her arm so that we might have written ourselves on her, hearts for "i's," 4EVA—our names the last thing she'd see before she fell asleep. We would have liked it if she could have trailed her char and sorrow through our lives endlessly. But by the time her family got a new house, she'd already folded back into us with little fanfare: mediocre Girl Scout, milk-spiller, spelling bee runner-up. Her kitten sweatshirt came to seem slightly sappy, her understated lisp suddenly impossible to ignore. Now and then we'd catch her face in the crowded bathroom mirror and shrug. Even so, we could not help pressing our fingers into the soft bellies of our carnival bears, our thin, dry voices whispering c-o-n-f-l-a-g-r-a-t-i-o-n.

Juveniles

At dawn, the birds storm
the backyard like a country
they are astonished to have
won without a single shot
fired. There is no end
to its richness, every seed
tasting like a year.
They have no superstitions.
They celebrate in
monosyllables.
They cannot feel the god
who lives in the wires
strung over our houses
no matter how tightly
they grasp him with their feet.
The sky is one long drink.
They will never know the quiet
hands with which we hold them
when we find them
under the hedge at dusk.

Nessun Dorma

The nurses' station was an offstage quartet
endlessly tuning up
as the late night greased my forehead.
I counted the blue fermatas on his gown
until their figures slurred.

Those hours were a beige braid of dementia
throughout which my grandfather
did not know my name, but cried out
help me help me help me
like the panicked bell of a buoy.

His ulcerous feet were propped and strapped
into quilted sheaths
like haughty coloraturas—
I was frightened by the ruin of his warped toes,
and because I was a coward, touched them.

I'd had terrible plans for the woman
in the framed Impressionist print above his bed,
her spattered face pinkly serene
over her piano. To draw out each note
she would surrender like a terrified wire.

You're hurting me, no matter
how gently I held his hand—though he may
have been talking to the light
that had crawled from under the curtains
and door to warp his face.

The oldest story is someone waiting for dawn.
A mouth opens in a reverse aria:
the last music rushes in.

The Poet Who Does Not Believe in Ghosts

walks through the darkened house
and knows she is alone

       the groans in the pipes are not secret
       communiqués meant for her deciphering

       the gnashing of the floorboards
       is just old wood badly joined

       there is no century-old vengeance
       reaching out from mirrors

       no floating ethereal feet
       advancing over the bedroom's threshold

       the branch tapping against the window
       is a branch tapping against the window

it is not that she has no fear
or that she is stubbornly logical

she believes death is God's apology
for suffering

a promise that the deepest human pain
will never be eternal

       the sudden cataclysms of the brain
       the helplessness of search parties

children savaged, watching one's beloved go mad
the slow betrayal of the body

it is death, and not the rainbow,
that is God's covenant with mankind

so you won't set us back upon the earth afterwards
transparent and helpless

singing out our griefs as we move
empty chairs about in empty rooms?

No   I would Never

so let her make her unpoetic way
through cobwebs and past unsettled curtains

let her be content that her mother her father are not
disturbing the genealogies of attic dust

the friends she's outlived are not circulating
damp manifestoes in the basement's shadows

they do not need her to solve anything
are not writing her letters to which she owes replies

let her be content that she is completely unnecessary
to her beloved dead

Because my grief was a tree

It forgave the dog that pissed on it
It moderated quarrels between the stones
It had a few knots that looked like a weeping face
It had a few knots that looked like a laughing face
It never stopped grasping the earth
It was badly tuned by the wind
It grew inedible fruit
It grew fruit that fed the worms magnificently
It held a yellow newspaper on its head for seven months
It felt the rumba in a squirrel's chest pressing against it
It wore a gash from when my friend was drunk and stupid
It looked up at the geese in their lofty arrows
It looked up at the geese in their trombone-heavy operettas
It looked up at the geese and wished them all good shoes
It stretched its arms wider every year
It waved its dozens of dark hats over the grass

Specimen #17

The pig's teeth in the cork-capped beaker rattle
bell-bright against the glass. They're as homely
as the animal itself: blunted, dun,
undecorative. But still, my small totems
against fear. Countless the times I've taken
one between my thumb and forefinger, rubbing
out a covert prayer of touch. Difficult
to explain this kind of comfort, or what
the nubs of bone may be murmuring to
the flesh-pads. Say that it's the reassurance
of the omnivore: we can't choose the feast
that will sustain us—our only power
is to greet the terrible and joyous
alike with our souls' most ravenous yes.

Revision

The dark anemone of hair clotting
the drain; a thumbnail's archeology
splintered in ravines of caulk; a dry tongue
of scab knotted in a whorl of TP.
Hello, little abandonments, hello.
There should be just enough of you to make
another me entirely by now —
a big doll of my dead stuff, cicatrix
grin and dandruff shadow. Or maybe not
the creepshow I think. Perhaps clean
and ageless, the dying already gotten
over with. Maybe a light flag, breathing
out in drafts, a loosened, papery tune
humming *again again again again.*

Notes

The epigraph for "Drag Day at Dollywood" comes from the 2016 *New York Times* article "Dolly Parton Is Proud of Her Gay Fans and Hillary Clinton" by Melena Ryzik.

"Cathy Dies" is for Amelia Campbell.

"Etymology" was inspired, in part, by Fernando Botero's 1989 painting *Melancholy*.

"Marlene Dietrich Plays Her Musical Saw for the Troops" and "Marlene Dietrich Considers Penicillin" are indebted to Donald Spoto's *Blue Angel: The Life of Marlene Dietrich*.

The quote preceding "Forged Medieval German Church Fresco with Clandestine Marlene Dietrich" comes from Noah Charney's 2014 article in *The Atlantic*, "Why So Many Art Forgers Want to Get Caught." Many poems in this book are indebted to Charney's *The Art of Forgery: The Minds, Motives and Methods of Master Forgers*, as well as Edward Dolnick's *The Forger's Spell: A True Story of Vermeer, Nazis, and the Greatest Art Hoax of the Twentieth Century*.

"Notes on the Village of Liars" is inspired by the poem "Notes on Pigs" from Jenny George's *The Dream of Reason*.

The sequence "The Stereoscopic Man" is inspired, in part, by René Magritte's *Portrait of Paul Nougé* (1927).

Regarding "Marlene Dietrich Meets David Bowie, 1978": Dietrich and Bowie filmed their shared scene in separate cities; they never met.

In "Marlene Dietrich Considers Penicillin, 1950," "Fleming" refers to Alexander Fleming, who discovered penicillin in 1928.

"Mating Call of the Re-Creation Panda" is inspired by Melissa Milgrom's *Still Life: Adventures in Taxidermy.* "The poet" is Marianne Moore.

The title of the poem "*Nessun Dorma*" is an aria from Puccini's posthumously completed 1926 opera *Turandot*. In memory of Samuel Hutchison Beer.

"The Poet Who Does Not Believe in Ghosts" is for Craig Arnold and Jake Adam York.

Acknowledgments

Some of these poems have appeared, sometimes in different forms, in the pages of the following publications. Many thanks to the editors, readers, and staff for their kind attention.

Alaska Quarterly Review
"Etymology"
"Scat"

American Poetry Review
"Self-Portrait as Duckie Dale"
"The Benevolent Sisterhood of Inconspicuous Fabricators"
"Because my grief was a tree"

Cherry Tree
"Two-Headed Taxidermied Calf"
"Dear Bruce Wayne,"

Crazyhorse
"Forged Medieval German Church Fresco with Clandestine
        Marlene Dietrich"
"Heart in Turmeric"

descant
"Revision"

Jet Fuel Review
"Elegy"
"Kindness/Kindling"
"*Nessun Dorma*"

Memorious
"Cathy Dies"

The New Yorker
"Juveniles"

Poetry
"The Magicians at Work"

The Rumpus
"The Plagiarist"

Southern Indiana Review
"Self-Portrait While Operating Heavy Machinery"

Southern Review
"Mating Call of the Re-Creation Panda"

Spillway
"Marlene Dietrich Plays Her Musical Saw for the Troops"
"Marlene Dietrich Considers Penicillin"

Texas Review
"Thorn Ostinato"
"Specimen #17"

Third Coast
"Small Claims Courtship"

Tupelo Quarterly
"Exclusive Interview"
"Notes on the Village of Liars"

Visible Binary
"Marlene Dietrich Meets David Bowie"

"The Demolitionists" was published as a limited edition broadside
by Croquet Press. Many thanks to Landon Godfrey and
Gary Hawkins.

"Still Life with Pork Livers Rolled Like Handkerchiefs" appeared
in the anthology *Still Life with Poem: Contemporary Natures
Mortes in Verse*. Many thanks to editors Jehanne Dubrow and
Lindsay Lusby.

"Revision" was awarded the 2013 Betsy Colquitt Poetry Award by
descant for the best poem or series of poems in an issue.

Heartfelt thanks . . .

To the writing communities of Denver and Colorado. Proud to call you my
friends, peers, and comrades.

To my wonderful colleagues in the University of Colorado Denver English
department and the Women's and Gender Studies program.

To MacDowell, where many of these poems were hatched, drafted, revised,
and futzed with in the midst of great beauty, calm, kinship, and support.
And bacon. And cake.

To queer weirdos who make art.

To Daniel Slager for giving this book such a fantastic home. And to all of the good folks at Milkweed for their talent, time, energy, and attention—not just for my work, but for all of the great authors and enterprises the press supports.

To Kelly Forsythe, for keeping my spirits up and giving wise advice over the years.

To Sandra Beasley, for invaluable feedback and insight.

To David Diaz, for all the Pueblo goodies!

To Nathan Oates, Amy Wilkinson, and Sylvie and Baxter; Katie Pierce, Mike Kardos, and Sam and Wyatt: may we always meet together on happy beaches. And an extra serving of thanks for Amy and Katie for brilliant poem feedback!

To Seth Brady Tucker and Olivia Tucker, and David J. Daniels and Neal Kawesch, for so much laughter and joy.

To Nicole Sealey and John Murillo, for all of the tables at which we've met in years past, and the many more to come.

To Sarah Hagelin and Jo Luloff, my dear, dear ladies. And to Will Buck, ya big lug.

To Miles Kahn and Elizabeth Nelson. Growing old and cranky with a pair of talented bums like you two is pretty great.

To Roo and Panda and their young rascals, as well as the entire Foster family.

To my family: the Talls, Colemans, Salisburys, Beers, Barkers, Davidsons, and all permutations and extrapolations thereof.

To Wayne Miller, Jeanne Ouellette, and Harper and Sean, for the many blessings you all bring to my life.

To Josh, Nicole, and Billie Rose Beer. I love you so fucking much.

To Maya Gurantz, for over twenty-five years of making art side by side together. My love and admiration for you is endless.

To Brian Barker. O my love, how precious is this life we have. I am grateful every day.

Dustin Moon

NICKY BEER is a bi/queer writer and the author of *The Diminishing House* and *The Octopus Game*, both winners of the Colorado Book Award for Poetry. Her honors include a fellowship from the National Endowment for the Arts, a MacDowell Fellowship, a Ruth Lilly Fellowship from the Poetry Foundation, and a fellowship and a scholarship from the Bread Loaf Writers' Conference. She is an associate professor at the University of Colorado Denver, where she serves as a poetry editor for *Copper Nickel*.

milkweed
editions

Founded as a nonprofit organization in 1980, Milkweed Editions is an independent publisher. Our mission is to identify, nurture and publish transformative literature, and build an engaged community around it.

Milkweed Editions is based in Bde Ota Othúŋwe (Minneapolis) within Mni Sota Makhoċhe, the traditional homeland of the Dakota people. Residing here since time immemorial, Dakota people still call Mni Sota Makhoċhe home, with four federally recognized Dakota nations and many more Dakota people residing in what is now the state of Minnesota. Due to continued legacies of colonization, genocide, and forced removal, generations of Dakota people remain disenfranchised from their traditional homeland. Presently, Mni Sota Makhoċhe has become a refuge and home for many Indigenous nations and peoples, including seven federally recognized Ojibwe nations. We humbly encourage readers to reflect upon the historical legacies held in the lands they occupy.

milkweed.org

Milkweed Editions, an independent nonprofit publisher, gratefully acknowledges sustaining support from our Board of Directors; the Alan B. Slifka Foundation and its president, Riva Ariella Ritvo-Slifka; the Amazon Literary Partnership; the Ballard Spahr Foundation; *Copper Nickel*; the McKnight Foundation; the National Endowment for the Arts; the National Poetry Series; the Target Foundation; and other generous contributions from foundations, corporations, and individuals. Also, this activity is made possible by the voters of Minnesota through a Minnesota State Arts Board Operating Support grant, thanks to a legislative appropriation from the arts and cultural heritage fund. For a full listing of Milkweed Editions supporters, please visit milkweed.org.

Interior design by Tijqua Daiker and Mary Austin Speaker
Typeset in Vendetta

Vendetta was designed in 1999 by John Downer. Inspired by the class of types
known as Venetian Old Style, Downer designed Vendetta while considering
the relationship between lowercase letters and capital letters in terms
of classical ideals and geometric porportions.
Vendetta can be characterized by
its synthesis of ideas,
old and new.